MAR 2016

TRIANGLE
A SLICE OF PIZZA OR A MOUNTAIN PEAK

By SYDNEY LEPEW

Illustrated by ANNIE WILKENSON

CANTATA
LEARNING
MANKATO, MINNESOTA

WWW.CANTATALEARNING.COM

CANTATA
LEARNING
MANKATO, MINNESOTA

Published by Cantata Learning
1710 Roe Crest Drive
North Mankato, MN 56003
www.cantatalearning.com

Library of Congress Control Number: 2014957017
978-1-63290-272-6 (hardcover/CD)
978-1-63290-424-9 (paperback/CD)
978-1-63290-466-9 (paperback)

Triangle: A Slice of Pizza or a Mountain Peak by Sydney LePew
Illustrated by Annie Wilkinson

Book design, Tim Palin Creative
Editorial direction, Flat Sole Studio
Executive musical production and direction, Elizabeth Draper
Music produced by Wes Schuck
Audio recorded, mixed, and mastered at Two Fish Studios, Mankato, MN

Printed in the United States of America.

VISIT

WWW.CANTATALEARNING.COM/ACCESS-OUR-MUSIC

TO SING ALONG TO THE SONG

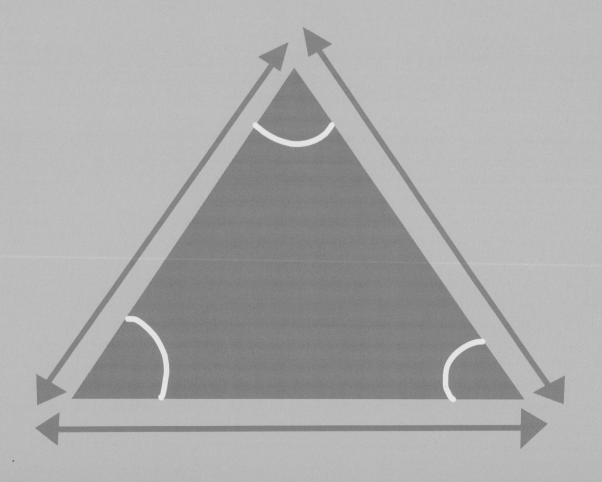

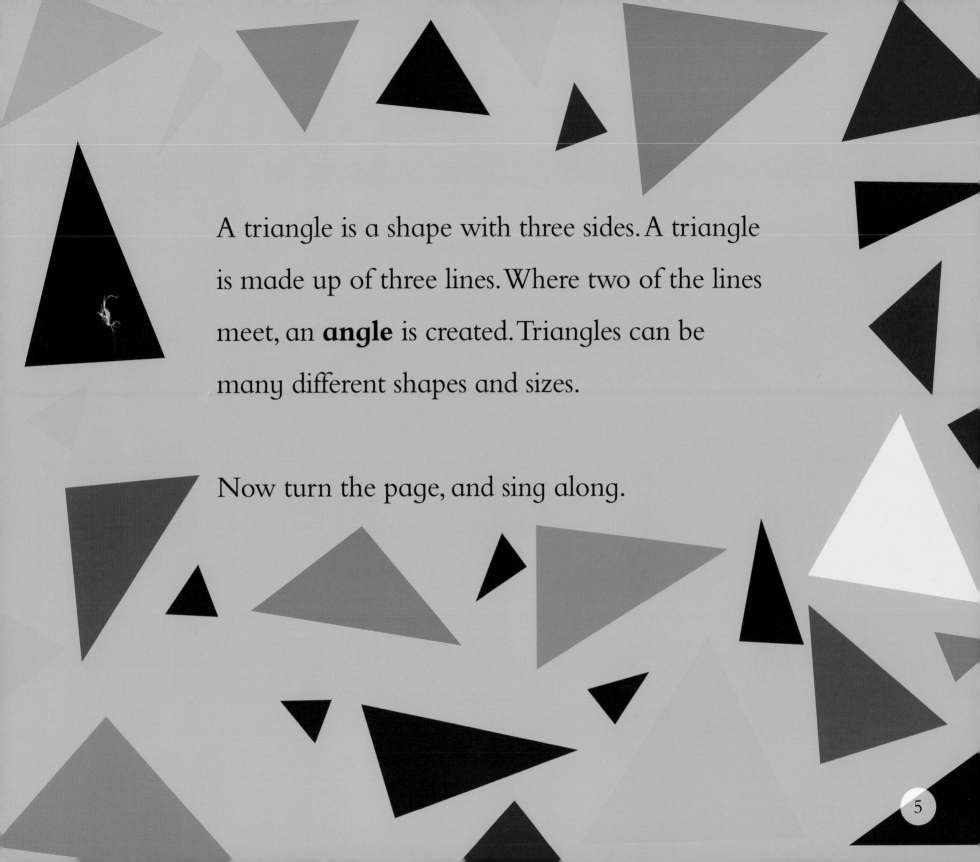

A triangle is a shape with three sides. A triangle is made up of three lines. Where two of the lines meet, an **angle** is created. Triangles can be many different shapes and sizes.

Now turn the page, and sing along.

5

Triangle, triangle, you have three sides.

You're a slice of pizza or a piece of pie.

You can be tall and thin or short and wide.

I'll find you triangle, wherever you hide.

You're the **peak** of a mountain way up high,
a **hang glider** flying across the sky,
the top of a house that we always drive by,
or half of a cheese sandwich. You can't hide!

9

There are all sorts of triangles, you know,

like streets signs, tall buildings, fancy windows.

The sails on a sailboat way out on the sea.

Just count their sides 1, 2, 3.

12

Triangle, triangle, you have three sides.

You're a slice of pizza or a piece of pie.

You can be tall and thin or short and wide.

I'll find you triangle, wherever you hide.

There are all kinds of shapes that surround us.
There's a circle and four-sided rhombus,
an oval, a square, a thin rectangle,
but none have three sides like a triangle.

Triangle, spell it with me.

T-R-I-A-N-G-L-E.

Triangle!

It's a tongue **tangle**.

18

Triangles can be big like the pyramids.

They can be small like a button or pin.

It doesn't matter if they're short or long.

They're important, so why don't you sing along.

PAPA PIZZERIA

20

Triangle, triangle, you have three sides.

You're a slice of pizza or a piece of pie.

You can be tall and thin or short and wide.

I'll find you triangle, wherever you hide.

YIELD

SONG LYRICS
Triangle: A Slice of Pizza or a Mountain Peak

Triangle, triangle, you have three sides.
You're a slice of pizza or a piece of pie.

You can be tall and thin or short and wide.
I'll find you triangle, wherever you hide.

You're the peak of a mountain way up high,
a hang glider flying across the sky,
the top of a house that we always drive by,
or half of a cheese sandwich. You can't hide!

There are all sorts of triangles, you know,
like streets signs, tall buildings, fancy
    windows.
The sails on a sailboat way out on the sea.

Just count their sides 1, 2, 3.

Triangle, triangle, you have three sides.
You're a slice of pizza or a piece of pie.

You can be tall and thin or short and wide.
I'll find you triangle, wherever you hide.

There are all kinds of shapes that
    surround us.
There's a circle and four-sided rhombus,
an oval, a square, a thin rectangle,
but none have three sides like a triangle.

Triangle, spell it with me.
T–R–I–A–N–G–L–E.
Triangle!
It's a tongue tangle.

Triangles can be big like the pyramids.
They can be small like a button or pin.
It doesn't matter if they're short or long.
They're important, so why don't you sing
    along.

Triangle, triangle, you have three sides.
You're a slice of pizza or a piece of pie.

You can be tall and thin or short and wide.
I'll find you triangle, wherever you hide.

Triangle: A Slice of Pizza or a Mountain Peak

Folk
Wes Schuck

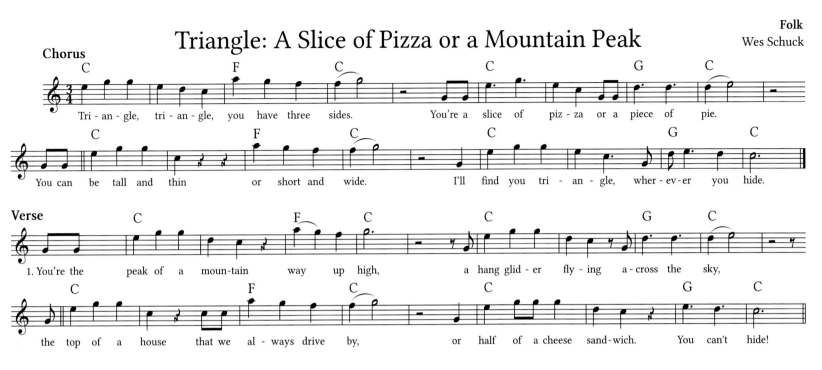

Chorus

Tri - an - gle, tri - an - gle, you have three sides. You're a slice of piz - za or a piece of pie.

You can be tall and thin or short and wide. I'll find you tri - an - gle, wher - ev - er you hide.

Verse

1. You're the peak of a moun-tain way up high, a hang glid - er fly - ing a - cross the sky,

the top of a house that we al - ways drive by, or half of a cheese sand-wich. You can't hide!

Verse 2
There are all sorts of triangles, you know,
like streets signs, tall buildings, fancy windows.
The sails on a sailboat way out on the sea.
Just count their sides 1, 2, 3.

Verse 3
There are all kinds of shapes that surround us.
There's a circle and four-sided rhombus,
an oval, a square, a thin rectangle,
but none have three sides like a triangle.

Chorus

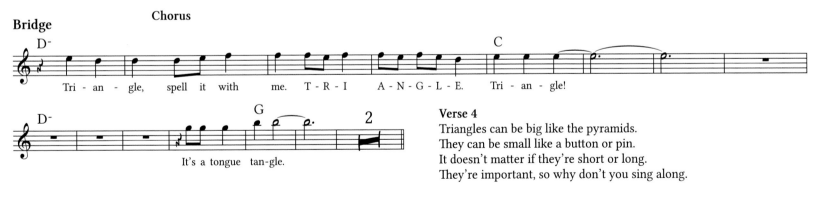

Bridge

Tri - an - gle, spell it with me. T - R - I A - N - G - L - E. Tri - an - gle!

It's a tongue tan-gle.

Verse 4
Triangles can be big like the pyramids.
They can be small like a button or pin.
It doesn't matter if they're short or long.
They're important, so why don't you sing along.

Chorus

GLOSSARY

angle—the space where two lines meet

hang glider—a small aircraft that is like a kite; a hang glider does not have an engine but uses wind to fly.

peak—the pointed top of a mountain

tangle—something that is twisted up

GUIDED READING ACTIVITIES

1. Draw a triangle. How many sides does a triangle have? Now try drawing a tall triangle. Then draw a short one.

2. Where have you seen triangles today?

3. How many triangles are in this book?

TO LEARN MORE

Aboff, Marcie. *If You Were a Triangle*. Minneapolis, MN: Picture Window Books, 2010.

Adler, David A. *Triangles*. New York: Holiday House, 2013.

Coss, Lauren. *Let's Sort Shapes*. Ann Arbor, MI: Cherry Lake Publishing, 2014.

Dilkes, D.H. *I See Triangles*. Berkeley Heights, NJ: Enslow Pub. 2011.